During the Level 4 Lockdown here in
New Zealand I used the time to imagine
what the enforced solitude might look
like for my friends and family. I wasn't
interested in the reality, that was hard
enough to deal with and there was more
than enough doom and gloom online and
in the news. No, I wanted to give them
spaces to inhabit that they might enjoy
and - while I was missing them - I wanted
to imagine them happy and at peace.

"Do what you can,
with what you have,
wherever you are."

Theodore Roosevelt

We had forgotten
how to just be quiet

My husband is a man of few words - in lockdown he missed the peace and solitude of the mountains.

His work includes shooting timelapse astronomical photography and I imagine there is nowhere more peaceful than the top of a mountain at night.

The Cushion Fort

What strange memories children
might well have of this time. Certainly
a lot of them seem to be dealing with
it better than the adults.

On Ye Nature of Rockes

Some people have always been happiest
in a quiet spot with their books, a dog and
their own company - like my friend,
Howard The Geologist.

Sedimentary Rockes and Ye character Thereof
On ye nature of Rockes
Part ye Second
GRANITES

"When life gives
you bubbles..."

This was for a friend who can genuinely
see the best in any situation. She has an
infectiously sunny outlook on life that
transmits to all those of us around her.

Beach Walk Bubbles

I missed our chocolate labrador very much during the lockdown. One ray of sunshine came from the news that lots of dogs were adopted as lockdown loomed. Hopefully they're still with their forever families.

Time to garden

We were so lucky in New Zealand that the weather through Lockdown, even though it was the middle of our winter, was mild and sunny. And, given the luxury of space which a lot of us enjoy here, a good proportion of us have gardens.

Kiwis scrubbed decks, weeded forgotten corners, tackled jobs around the house and reduced the never-ending To Do List. My gardening friend took the opportunity to take her mind off things and do some "garden meditation". She lost her gorgeous old dog not too long ago and now has a sprightly rescue pup to keep amused, so he must have been happy to be helping with the heavy work.

The Tree House

Another friend, based down south in NZ, loves her garden and values her quiet times for work, for creative thinking and just getting away from it all.

Creative thinking is an odd beast; you can't force it and it seems to come from a part of the brain that works best when you are walking the dog, weeding, taking a hike or going for a swim.

At any rate, doing something hypnotic and rhythmic seems to allows your brain to relax, sideline the relentless everyday background chatter and produce creative ideas.

The She Shed

A love of animals and her family is what makes another southern friend one of the most lovely people I know. She is genuinely kind and sees the good in people.

Her special place would not be private, I think, but would be open-season for all the animals on the property - a welcoming bolt hole where you would always have an soft ear to 'scroffle' while you enjoyed a glass of wine.

Please welcome my Brother's Bear on Bongos

When I asked my brother in the UK where his happy place might be this is what he asked for. He noodles endlessly on his guitar, plugged in so we can't hear what he's up to, and over the years has become very accomplished though he is shy about playing in front of us.

Of course everyone needs a mate to accompany them so why not a bongo-playing bear...?

Away from everything

One of my UK friends was heavily involved with the reponse to the virus and worked, with her husband, a GP in rural England, through the lockdown to keep as many people safe as they could. When I spoke to her I could hear her anxiety, determination to do the right thing and basic human goodness coming through her exhaustion.

I thought she deserved a room, painted her favourite colour, where she could sit in a comfy chair, by the fire, with her lovely dog, Fred and the memory of her little cat Fluffy who had recently died. With a bottle of her favourite gin on hand too.

Beach memories

Losing animals is heartbreaking. I painted
this for my friend who lost her huge,
characterful black dog during lockdown.
He was such a big personality, loved the
beach and barked relentlessly until the
ball was thrown for him, over and over
- he never seemed to tire of dashing into
the waves to retrieve it. We all loved him.

The Magnificent Shed

Not just your run-of-the-mill shed!
A shed of such magnificence that it
featured in New Zealand's grandest
lifestyle magazine. Made from recycled,
re-purposed and found materials by two
friends of ours - and to the very highest
standards, I predict that this shed will
be standing long after the house on the
property has crumbled to dust. A true
work of art that gives my friend joy
every time she enters it.

Mapua Easter Fair

Of course the Mapua Easter Fair couldn't happen in 2020. It's the biggest one day event in the whole of The South Island and is run entirely by volunteers to raise money for the local school and playcentre.

We were well on with the preparations and I had drawn a lot of sketches to refresh the publicity material we had been using for years. This bunny needed a mask to deliver the message that the Fair was not going ahead. And our PM, Jacinda, announced that the Easter Bunny was an essential worker so he could get on with his job!

A Love of Animals

I despair of humanity when I see what animals go through - and then there are rays of light from people who go above and beyond to care for them, mend them and just love them.

Barista Cats - recently renamed Purrs and Beans is the only Auckland café where you can get a good coffee (best coffee in the world here in NZ!) and also a cat or kitten cuddle. What could be better? You pay a small entry fee which goes towards the cats' welfare and upkeep and they have a foster-room. One day I will visit for sure.

Fisherman

I have long suspected that this is
actually what fishermen get up
to all day...

The Bird Lady

An artist friend of mine has won
multiple awards for her pastel paintings
of animals and birds. Somehow, with
a pastel pencil, she can make a snow
leopard so soft you want to stroke it and
a kereru so fat and sleek that he looks
as though the branch will break under
his weight. She lives in a quiet valley
overlooking a river and seems to be
living her best life, as they say.

Otters In Bubbles

Though there are none in New Zealand, and thankfully us idiot humans haven't seen fit to introduce them, I do love otters. Of all the animals, they are the ones who look as though they are having the most fun.

Night on the Sea

There is nothing more peaceful than a calm night, with my animals, looking out to sea. It puts all problems at least into perspective if not actually fixed and makes you acknowledge that life delivers both good and bad, happy and sad and that's just how it is. Amor Fati as the stoics say - "embrace your fate".

Another Perfect Studio

In an ancient building with thick stone walls, a fire for winter, cool in the summer. A window out onto a wild, herb-fragranced garden that somehow gardens itself. A big sleeping cat, flat out on some very expensive watercolour paper (they have a knack of doing that...). No devices, no mobile phones but perhaps something that I might listen to the odd podcast on.

Mermaid Bubbles

There is a worldwide creative project that takes place in May every year called MerMay. Artists - anyone at all in fact - all over the world paint or draw a mermaid from their imagination and post it online, or not, there are really no rules and it is just for fun. You can do one a day for the month or one - or none!

Given that the world was in lockdown - or not, depending on where you were - the submissions were poignant, nostalgic, angry, political and just downright beautiful, every sort of mermaid you can imagine. Of course, mine featured otters.

CPSIA information can be obtained
at www.ICGtesting.com
Printed in the USA
LVHW071946091120
671181LV00003B/6

9 780473 543440